Wrong Way Peach Fuzz:

A Turtle Tale

by Kirsten Dahlen

ISBN 978-1-4357-1273-7

Copyright © 2008 by Kirsten Dahlen

Cover photo © 1998 by Kirsten Dahlen

Back Cover photo © 2005 by Megh Freeland

For Megh, Tom and Gabe, who believed in me when I had forgotten the magic of the sea.

and

For sea turtles everywhere: may they grace our seas, and our lives, for generations to come.

Prologue

Waving a white starched bed sheet like a matador flagging a bull, Andy yelled, "If we all work together, we can drag this through the water like a net. Then, we can lift her out of the pool."

"That's a great idea. Who wants to help?" Anna asked the crowd. Women kicked off their heels, men shucked their sports coats and rolled up their shirtsleeves, and kids dove for a hold on the sheet. Everyone wanted to help rescue Peach Fuzz from the small pool.

This should be a snap, I thought, after organizing the rescue party. Anna, Andy and I slowly lowered the sheet into the deep end of the pool. We clumsily dragged it through the water, intending to catch Peach Fuzz as if she were a giant fish. Nicola and Lamar used a broom handle to coax the wayward sea turtle into a corner of the swimming pool where she would be easier to trap. Just as we were about to nab her, Peach Fuzz dodged our makeshift net and darted to the other end of the concrete ocean. Could the turtle really know that we were trying to capture her?

We regrouped and tried again as the children shooed her into another corner, offering treats no turtle had ever tried. Surely, she would want some cookies and pizza, right? Peach Fuzz did not seem interested, but she swam along obediently. Perhaps she was looking for a way to escape the sheer tiled walls on her own power.

Hopes were high as the sheet closed in on the sea turtle a second time. However, at the last minute, Peach Fuzz gracefully avoided the net, like an elegant, underwater ballet dancer. She seemed to think this was some sort of game.

"Maybe the third time's the charm." I said, as we got ready to try again. Peach Fuzz got away that time too. I shrugged and looked at Anna for advice and encouragement.

Her face looked as troubled as my own. "I guess we just have to keep trying," Anna said optimistically. Peach Fuzz continued to swim away from us, again and again, for over an hour. We didn't expect to catch her on the first try, but this was getting ridiculous! It was beginning to feel like we were taking an aerobics class in the muggy night air.

The crowd of resort guests continued to cheer for Peach Fuzz. It all seemed like part of the vacation experience for them: a personal Sea World with Peach Fuzz as the star attraction. Anna and I were worried though. We knew how important it was to return the turtle to the safety of the sea. If she remained in the pool, she would release her eggs underwater, drowning them. If she stayed in too long, she would starve to death. That was simply unacceptable. We would get the turtle out even if we had to jump in the pool and wrestle with her. I wanted to avoid that as the 140-pound turtle was a lot bigger than I was. Even Anna and I together would be challenged by the size and strength of the trapped turtle. Peach Fuzz had powerful limbs, a snapping jaw and strong claws. No one really wanted to go swimming with the scared animal.

All of our activity woke up the nighttime beach. A confused mourning dove cooed from its rooftop roost. A flock of small bananaquits chirped excitedly in the trees, flying towards us in a burst of energy, jarring our already stressed nerves. Startled lizards scurried across the pool deck. Mosquitoes buzzed around our ears, biting our exposed arms and legs. Our hands were raw where the soggy sheet had rubbed against wet, tender skin. Our eager volunteers were changing to spirited observers as their fatigue took a toll. I was frustrated, hot and cranky. More than anything, I was worried that we wouldn't be able to get the sea turtle out of the pool. My temper was growing short.

It seemed strange that I had grown so attached to this particular animal so quickly. Anna and I had arrived in Antigua just three months ago. We met Peach Fuzz a few weeks later, but she had already worked her way into my heart. Now, I was worried that I would fail to save her from her watery prison. How could I live with myself if this turtle died while I was supposed to be protecting her and her nests?

The Arrival

Beneath our plane, the Caribbean Sea winked with white and silver light as it reflected the intense rays of the midday sun. Tiny islands appeared on the horizon like a necklace of small jade stones in an impossibly clear blue sea. Antigua's northeast coast slowly rose from the water as we made our final approach to the VC Bird International Airport. Patches of deep green mangrove, interspersed with beaches of cream-colored sand, dotted the coast, thinning to dry grassland and palm trees on higher ground. Anna and I were about to arrive in paradise. One of those small gems would soon be our home.

Earlier that spring morning, Anna's parents had driven us to the Philadelphia airport a thousand miles to the north. We put on brave faces for our families, talking of the adventure that lay ahead, but in reality, we were terrified. We were leaving behind everything we knew to spend a year here, living and working with the endangered Hawksbill sea turtles that nested in this remote island nation.

As the plane landed, Anna and I held our breath and looked to each other for reassurance. Anna gave me a crooked smile, as if to say, "Ready or not, here we go…" We were both so nervous! We didn't know anyone in this small Eastern Caribbean nation. Even our boss, Jim, was home in the United States. What were we thinking? I hadn't even heard of Antigua until about a year ago, and now I was here to stay. As the reality of our move sunk in, I had a sudden craving for the familiar things of home – frozen yogurt, HBO and my mother's not so wonderful cooking sounded strangely appealing.

The ground crew wheeled a rickety metal staircase to the side of the plane and the flight attendant opened the plane's sealed door, introducing us to the torpid tropical heat. Anna and I gathered our carry-on luggage and walked forward; it felt as if we were walking the plank. Our hair and clothing seemed to wilt as we approached the open doorway, about to step into our future. While we knew the expectations and demands of our work, we had no idea what to expect of life in the islands. Would we be welcome? Would we make friends? Would life here be as happy as the commercials for island vacations always suggest? As I set foot on the stairway, my stomach was doing flip-flops. I was full of fear of the unknown. Would I regret making a commitment to live and work here for the next year?

"Anna, Kirsten, welcome to Antigua!"

A deep voice from the waiting crowd startled both of us, calling our names as soon as we stepped off the plane into the blazing sunlight. I scanned the small group waiting near the pink, two-story airport, trying to determine who could possibly know our names. Had someone from the resort come to meet us? Was it that obvious that we were the new "Turtle Girls"? With our conservative clothing and tense manner, we did stick out from the planeload of happy tourists who had traveled with us. Everyone else on board was clad in an array of Bermuda shorts, Hawaiian shirts, sundresses and sandals, eager to find their place in the sun. Anna and I were the only ones who didn't look as if we were on vacation.

Our new island 'father' John, and his wife, Sarah, waved to us from across the tarmac. We had not met them before, but they had worked with our professor, Jim, back at the University of Georgia for many years. Jim told us to turn to them if we needed help while in the country, but we had not expected them to meet our flight. Their presence was instantly reassuring, and I breathed a sigh of relief. The logistics of getting all of our belongings through customs and out to our island had been on my mind. It seemed we had some ready-made friends to help us adjust to life in Antigua.

As we reached the pavement, the tropical heat rose in waves from the hot tar, mixed with the stale jet fuel exhaust, and engulfed us in a grimy embrace. John and Sarah came to the rescue, taking our carry-ons and shepherding us towards the new airport. The sturdy concrete building, flanked with graceful palms, served as a welcome mat for the island. As we entered the glass doors, the air conditioning felt like heaven.

Anna and I spent the next thirty minutes grabbing all of our gear from the rotating belt in the baggage claim area, throwing it onto two large carts. John laughed, "Do you think you have enough stuff?" He was clearly stunned by our mountains of luggage. Anna and I had scuba gear, bicycles, and suitcases in unwieldy piles that threatened to tumble to the tile floor. A toddler, clutching his stuffed dinosaur, tugged on his father's hand as he inched away from our towering bags. His father looked at us with wide eyes as he carried on a lively conversation with two resort porters. They must have been relieved they didn't have to carry our gear.

"A year is a long time. We didn't want to forget anything important," I said, trying to defend myself. I didn't want to admit that half of our supplies were probably unnecessary and I didn't know John yet, or his sense of humor. "Jim sent a lot of stuff from the University too." John and Sarah eyed each other knowingly as they grabbed our carts, steering us towards the Customs officials.

"Where is Jim?" Sarah asked, "He usually comes down to help train the team."

"Jim trained us a few years ago in Georgia, so he decided not to come this time," Anna replied.

Anna and I met two years earlier when we both spent the summer training as sea turtle biologists in Georgia. We worked through long, buggy nights in the dense, still air of a southern summer, listening to tree frogs sing in the pine forests, fishing for flounder and shrimp, running away from lightening storms and experiencing the joys and trials of field work. We learned well from our mentor and Anna and I became good friends. We were continuing our turtle adventures again on this enchanting island in the Caribbean Sea.

As we arrived at the Customs counter, two officials asked us to load all of our bags onto the conveyor belt, rolling their eyes and giggling at our overloaded carts. "You want to search through everything?" Anna asked apprehensively. "That could take hours!"

After our long journey, we were relieved to learn they were just kidding. As a well-known barrister in the country, John was able to smooth our way through Customs and Immigration without too much trouble. We were officially welcomed as scientists and guests, free to explore our new home.

"Well, let's get back to the house. There isn't another boat to Jumby Bay until tomorrow, so you'll stay with us." With that, Sarah and John bundled all of our bags and the two of us into their waiting car. There was hardly room left for John to see out of the rear window as he backed out of his parking space. Anna and I were happy to be out of the airport and settled in with the Fullers. We were starting to believe this would be a great year.

As we drove along the winding beachfront road to their home in Hodges Bay, John and Sarah told us about how they met Jim, and how this sea turtle project was born.

John loved to boat and fish offshore. His family had lived here for generations and owned one of the smaller islands near where we would live. While out fishing, John often noticed strange marks on the sandy pocket beaches. Local sea turtle fishermen told him these were crawls left by nesting Hawksbill sea turtles. Knowing that these animals were hunted to near extinction, John was eager to bring in an expert to study and protect the small group of turtles that he had discovered on Long Island, or Jumby Bay. That's why he first invited Jim to the island in 1987.

Along with the University of Georgia, John, Sarah and Jim designed this project to protect the nesting turtles and their eggs, hoping to rebuild a population that was growing smaller every year.

Since then, there have been teams of biologists on the beach during every nesting season. Anna and I were just the most recent pair working to increase our understanding of these animals.

We soon arrived at the gate to John and Sarah's rambling island home. As we drove over the bumpy grating, Anna and I were both confused – they lived on a hill, so why did they need a drainage grate at the end of the driveway? "John, do you really get enough rain here to need that grate? I thought Antigua was a pretty dry place," Anna commented.

John chuckled as Sarah explained, "It's not for the rain, it's for the goats and cows. We don't want them grazing in the garden." Now that Sarah mentioned it, I had seen many farm animals wandering along the roadways. While most of these animals had brands and some dragged chains behind them, they were not in fenced pastures. Islanders kept the animals from grazing in their gardens with fences and grates that made it hard for the animals to cross without getting their hooves caught. I'd never heard about that in a Club Med commercial!

The Fuller's home slowly emerged from the lush gardens as we drove through the entrance. It was a traditional wooden island house, sturdy and open to the wind. Deep porches and covered walkways joined the main two-story teak house to small, one-room sleeping wings. Gauzy mosquito nets floated over beds and reading areas that were open to the trade winds. The design allowed cooling breezes to circulate throughout the house, cutting down on air-conditioning and energy costs. It was elegant in its simplicity, and clearly a much-loved retreat from the real world. A small one-room schoolhouse, nestled in the dense green and pink garden, served as their guest room. The chalkboards and desks had been replaced with day beds and British antiques, creating a charming atmosphere for the weary traveler.

While John was showing us to our rooms, Sarah started the evening meal. After a dinner of fresh caught flying fish and wahoo, we decided to go for a swim. I felt as if I'd stepped into a travel brochure as we walked out the door to my room onto the coral-rock path to the pool. Oleander, bougainvillea and fig trees dominated the walkway, providing shade and vibrant tropical color. This private oasis was a great escape from the dust and dirt of our long journey. The cooling dip in the pool was just what I needed to unwind my tired muscles and help me relax. Sleep came easily as I lay in my mosquito net canopy, thinking about the year ahead, and slowly allowing my anxiety and fear to slip away.

After a much-needed rest, Anna and I woke up to the warm, clear light of a Caribbean sunrise. It looked like it had rained frangipani petals in the yard overnight. The gardener raked the soft white flowers as if they were fallen leaves in a northern autumn, crushing them and releasing their crisp, clean scent. Bananaquits and mourning doves sang in the trees as the sun shone through the bougainvillea-covered porch. Though I could have stayed there for hours, the scent of fresh-baked bread jolted both Anna and I out of our beds in a search for food.

After breakfast, John and Sarah spent the morning showing us around the island. The Fullers wanted us to know how to find our way around before sending us off on our new adventure. I was looking forward to getting rid of that starry-eyed tourist glow. I had to learn to live here, not just vacation, and needed to know how things worked in my new country.

The early morning was a riot of color and noise in the tropical heat. Brightly painted houses and flowering trees dotted the roadways, making the island seem like a living postcard. Goats wandered freely, bleating incessantly, and chewing on grass, bushes and laundry hung out to dry. There were cows everywhere, blocking traffic and sunning on the sand at Jabberwocky Beach. Animated locals piled into minivans by the dozen on their morning commute. Apparently, the American perception of 'personal space' was not a recognized requirement here.

We arrived at the newly minted Wood Center shopping plaza far too quickly—I was enjoying the ride through the countryside and was jolted back to reality at the sight of the grocery store and post office. I was hoping for something with a little more charm; this looked like a small piece of the US, relocated to paradise. Strangely, security in the grocery was tight – guards stood at the end of every aisle, laughing as Anna and I loaded a cart with every conceivable food available in our quest to stock our new home. We were amused to find mushrooms from a farm back in Pennsylvania in Anna's hometown. This really was a small world.

Once we'd finished our more mundane grocery shopping and assorted errands, John and Sarah set out to teach us about the tourist hotspots in Antigua. We toured a former sugar plantation called "Betty's Hope" so we could better understand the island's British Colonial history. The coral rock stumps of sugar mills and windmills dotted the hills across the island; it wasn't until we saw the museum quality pieces at Betty's Hope that we understood their meaning. Like most of the region, Antigua had a past steeped in the perils of the sugar and rum trades, capitalizing on their investment in human bondage. What a terrible era that must have been for the people who tilled the soil in the torpid, dense heat. No mention was made of the lives and bodies destroyed by the colonial juggernaut. These more troubling pieces of history are easy to ignore when you're in town just to enjoy the sun and sand.

John and Sarah also showed us a remote site where we could find beads and pottery created centuries ago by the native Arawaks, and the natural "Devil's Bridge" created by thousands of years of pounding waves on the islands eastern coast. Antigua was a rich and diverse country, with much more to explore than the three hundred sunny beaches the travel agents all advertised. Anna and I felt much more comfortable after meeting our new 'parents' and learning our way around the island. We were eager to see all the hidden treasures here, but saved the rest for another day.

At noon, John and Sarah took us to a hidden dock, tucked in the mangroves behind a small hotel. While standing under the vibrant green trees, waiting for our boat to arrive, Anna and I saw our new home in the distance. Jumby Bay Island was only three miles away, but it seemed so remote, as we left behind our new Antiguan family. Little did we know that we were just beginning an adventure we would touch our hearts and change our lives.

Anna and I first met Wrong Way Peach Fuzz about a month after our arrival on Jumby Bay. The sea turtle would earn her name later in the summer, after she had shown a remarkable ability to get lost on the island. The wandering turtle would wind up in some unusual places during the nesting season. She seemed to go every way but the right way; by the end of the summer, she would show us all the way home.

Hunting Turtle Tracks

Anna and I went to work on our very first night on Jumby Bay. We were eager to see our first Hawksbill sea turtle nest, and hoped there might even be some hatchlings from a nest laid earlier in the spring. As we prepared to go to the beach for the night, we looked out across our front yard to the wide, white palm-shaded beaches and the gentle rocking waves of the Caribbean Sea. This beach would be our "office" for nearly a year. I could tell we would be spoiled by this experience; no other employment would ever be as rewarding as this would be for the two of us.

We had made a commitment to work every night for the next eight months, walking the length of Pasture Bay Beach once an hour, from sunset to sunrise. The beach was only about 500 yards long, but walking through the soft sand in all sorts of weather would challenge our strength, stamina and resolve. It was our mission to find every turtle that crawled onto this beach from the sea to lay her eggs.

I was worried about failing to meet our professional goals and expectations. What would happen to this valuable project if we overlooked one of the turtles? It usually took about ninety minutes for a turtle to nest before returning to the sea. What if I fell asleep, or went home for a cup of coffee at the wrong time? The fear of failure was enough to keep me awake through that first long night.

The turtles we were looking for were hawksbill turtles that returned to Pasture Bay Beach to nest every other year. During nesting years, these turtles will visit the beach every two weeks until they have laid about five nests, each with around 100 to 150 ping-pong ball sized eggs. This is a big job for a turtle. She has to leave her home in the sea, crawl up the sandy beach, dig a deep hole in the sand, lay her eggs, fill the hole back in with sand and disguise the nest so that predators, like dogs and raccoons, can't find it. It's a difficult job for her that requires strength and perseverance. It would be like wriggling up the beach on your belly and trying to dig a 20-inch deep hole with your feet, every two weeks, all summer long! It's just as hard for a hawksbill sea turtle, who is more accustomed to swimming in the open ocean than trying to navigate on land. After all of this hard work, the mother sea turtle returns to the sea. She will come back in about two weeks to repeat the process, but she will most likely never see her eggs, or her hatchlings, again.

Most sea turtles nest at night when the beach is cooler under the cover of darkness. This means we have to stay up all night if we want to find nesting sea turtles as they crawl out of the sea to lay their eggs. It is more difficult than it sounds to switch from living during the day to working at night. We go to sleep with the sun, and rise at noon when it grows too warm and bright for rest, even in air-conditioned rooms. There are benefits to this, though, as it would be much harder to work outdoors all day in the strong sunlight and scorching temperatures of the Caribbean summer. Anna and I were able to spend those hours in cool comfort, though it was hard to stay indoors at all when we could be outside, playing in the ocean, looking for lizards and butterflies on the island or exploring the near-by coral reefs. We were never still for very long, thinking that we could always catch up on lost sleep when we returned to the US.

****

One June evening, a few hours after sunset, Anna and I walked down the beach, our feet sinking nearly ankle deep in dry sand that stuck to our feet and sandals. Gentle trade winds blew through our hair, tangling it and convincing us it was time to start wearing ponytails. Waves crashed against the near-shore reef. We walked under a flood of starlight as the tropical night wrapped us in its warm embrace. The scent of the fresh, salty tang of the sea, mixed with coconuts and frangipani flowers, floated on the breeze. Anna sang softly as we walked along the beachfront.

We scoured the shoreline carefully, looking for signs of sea turtles. Soon, we noticed what looked like wide tire tracks in the sand. A sea turtle leaves these tracks, called a "crawl," when she emerges from the ocean and pulls herself up the beach with her flippers, dragging her heavy body over the sand.

As our eyes followed the tracks on the beach, Anna and I could see that the turtle had already crawled above the high tide line, where she could find a dry site for her nest. Anna and I quietly crept further up the beach until we saw an adult sea turtle near the top of a small sand dune. In the dim moonlight, we could see that she was still digging her nest, flinging sand high in the air. We went back down towards the water's edge and waited for her to finish.

****

If we disturb a sea turtle while she is digging her nest, she may react by returning to the safety of the sea to escape any possible predators on the beach. Anna and I knew that any noise, light or sudden movement from us could scare her and make her go back to the ocean without laying her eggs. Since the turtle had already put so much effort into crawling up the beach and beginning to dig her nest, we didn't want her to leave before she had completed her task.

We were here to protect the nesting turtles, their nests, and their hatchlings. When the nesting turtle started to lay her eggs in a few minutes, she would enter a trance-like state, seeming to need all of her energy to lay her eggs. At this point, we could do our work without disturbing the mother turtle.

****

Anna and I listened to her toss sand out of the nest cavity as she continued to build her nest that evening. She often threw sand so high it hit an overhanging tree, with a sound like heavy rain falling through the forest. While we waited until it was safe to go see the turtle, we sat on the beach together, a few yards from the turtle, and searched for constellations in the clear night sky. Anna was terrific at finding these complicated star patterns, but I couldn't find even the simplest ones, so we mostly played dot-to-dot with the stars and invented names for our new constellations. It may not be very scientific, but it was a fun way to pass the time while we waited for the sea turtle to begin to lay her eggs.

When we couldn't hear the sea turtle throwing sand anymore, we crawled slowly back up the dune and found her near the base of a small sea grape tree. Her rear flippers were curling up at the edges a few times each minute, so we knew she had begun laying her eggs. She had entered her nesting "trance" and was unlikely to respond to any noise or activity around her. That meant it was now safe for us to work without causing her to leave the beach.

We gently measured the length and width of her carapace, or shell, and flippers with a tape measure. Then, we examined her for injuries, tags, or tag scars. The chestnut-brown, leathery skin on her flippers had already dried after her long crawl up the beach. It was smooth and firm to the touch, and contrasted starkly with the orange-yellow color of the softer, wrinkled skin around her neck and tail. It was almost like running my hand over small, flat pebbles as I felt along her limbs for scars and old tags. She sighed heavily as she lay on the beach, depositing her eggs in the hole beneath her tail. The light from our flashlights shone on the mottled brown and gold scutes on her shell that were lightly dusted with coarse, white sand. It was easy to see why these beautiful scutes were used to make jewelry long ago. As we looked into her eyes, it looked like our turtle was crying, but Anna and I knew this was just the way a sea turtle gets rid of excess salt from her body.

She was small for a nesting sea turtle at 32 inches, and about 140 pounds, but that was within normal range. She was a young adult turtle who would continue to grow throughout most of her life. We were happy to discover that she had not been tagged before. This meant she was a neophyte sea turtle and that this was probably her very first nest.

"Anna, can you hand me some flipper tags?" Anna's long brown hair tangled in the breeze as she reached into her backpack for the Ziploc full of turtle tags. "I think this is a first-time nester. She seems small, but she's absolutely beautiful. There's not a scratch on her." Anna handed me two silvery metal tags as I sat beside the turtle.

It had been a blistering day on this Caribbean island, and we were grateful for the cooler evening air. As I tagged the turtle in her front flippers, taking care to be as gentle as possible, I called out the tag numbers to Anna: "This is PPX 683. What a dreary name for such a charmer. We can come up with something better than that."

"What do you think of 'Peach Fuzz'? The color of her neck and tail reminds me of fresh summer peaches. She is a cutie," Anna suggested.

"Sounds good to me." Little did we know that we had just met the animal that would be both our greatest challenge and our greatest joy over the next few months.

Once Peach Fuzz finished laying her eggs, she filled in the rest of the hole with more sand, carefully patting it down by lifting and dropping her bodyweight on the beach. She further camouflaged the nest by tossing sand in a six-foot wide arc so it was hard to find again. After her nest was well disguised, she turned toward the sea and crawled back to her ocean home. We had completed all our work with her, and it was time to say goodbye. We hoped we would see her on the beach laying another clutch in about two weeks.

****

Sea turtles come to shore to nest for a very long time. One loggerhead sea turtle from Little Cumberland Island has nested every other year for over 27 years! Tags such as the ones on Peach Fuzz and on turtles around the world help scientists follow the behavior of individual turtles and learn more about sea turtle biology. Flipper tags help to identify turtles when they arrive on a nesting beach, to track their growth and behavior over the years, and to determine how many hatchlings they have. When we tag a turtle, we place an inch-long, numbered, silver clip on the edge of her front flipper. It pinches a little when we are placing them on the turtle, kind of like getting your ears pierced.

Sometimes, flipper tags fall off, just like earrings, and we lose the identity and history of the animal along with the tag. For this reason, we also drill a unique pattern of holes in the scutes on the very back edge of a sea turtle shell. This pattern looks a lot like the dots on a pair of dice. It doesn't hurt the turtles at all. Their scutes, or scales, are made of keratin, just like your fingernails. Creating this pattern probably feels about the same as trimming your nails. As long as you don't get too close to your finger, or to the turtles flesh, there's no pain at all. We are always very careful to protect our turtles as much as possible.

Who Wants to Swim?

Anna and I walked the beach attentively, all night, every night, checking for signs of adult sea turtles crawling out of the ocean or hatchling sea turtles emerging from nests laid earlier in the year. Sometimes, the nighttime beach felt like a lonely, empty playground, eerily quiet except for the sound of the crashing waves and the wind in the trees. While Anna and I were good friends, it was easy to get bored with each other after so many hours alone together.

We invited everyone we met to join us on the beach, but most people were only visiting Jumby Bay for a few nights while on holiday. Our most constant friends were people who worked or owned vacation homes on the island. They enjoyed meeting the nesting turtles, making sand castles by moonlight and helping us search for tiny, inch-long baby sea turtles. It takes about 60 days for a nest, or clutch, to hatch. We were always eager to find the wriggling hatchlings. They're like little wind-up toys, constantly paddling their flippers as if swimming, even when we pick them up.

We never knew if we'd be able to share a nesting event with our guests, but we tried to invite them when we expected a turtle. Anna and I kept a chart in our kitchen with information about all of the turtles who came to lay their eggs on our beach. It helped us keep track of when we were expecting a visit from a turtle who had come earlier that summer, or when it was time for a nest to hatch.

Lamar was one of our most frequent visitors on Pasture Bay Beach. He had adopted us as his surrogate children to as his family lived in Dominica, a few hundred miles to the south. He chose to work as security here because pay rates were much higher in Antigua – he mailed money home once a month and visited his children twice a year. He took great care protecting us and coaching us on island etiquette. Anna quickly grew tired of his sometimes overbearing lectures, and would leave the beach when she saw his golf-cart at the beach entrance. I felt too guilty to leave; I knew he was lonely and needed to speak with someone. I didn't think he was very interested in the turtles, but it was nice to have company during the long night. Lamar was always full of stories. For such a big bear, he was a superstitious sweetheart.

After walking the beach until midnight one night, Anna and I were lounging on the beach chairs trying to decide if one of us should go home early for a little extra sleep. The distant sound of a small engine ended the conversation – Lamar was here to patrol the beach and chat. I said goodnight to Anna, knowing she would appreciate the chance to escape. As she cycled off to our teak and tile house, I stood to wrap myself in the sheet I often carried with me. The mosquitoes were bad that night and the trade winds were a little chilly at that late hour. The sheet worked as both bug spray and blanket.

I settled in to wait for Lamar to wander to my end of the beach, but it was a long wait. After about ten minutes, I walked up the beach a little to see if I could pick his form out in the dim moonlight, but I couldn't see anything. I heard the engine fire up as he drove away. Weird. He always wants to talk, especially late at night when there was nothing going on to occupy his time. I was sorry to see him go, and decided to go check on him at the guard office after I checked the beach for turtles. As long as I was back within an hour, I wouldn't miss any animals.

I biked across the island's brick paths to the resort dock. Lamar was in the tidy guardhouse, reading his paper. He glanced up as he heard the rattle of my bike chain, then quickly ducked behind the door. Very strange. What was going on with Lamar?

"Lamar, are you okay?" I called into the small room.

"Oh, turtle girl, it's you," Lamar replied.

"Of course it's me. Who else is awake at this hour?" I walked into his office to claim a seat and chat for a few minutes. "We saw your cart at the beach earlier, but you never came out. Did something happen on the island?"

"No, there's nothing going on. I just decided not to check the beach."

"Well, that's funny. Why drive all the way over there if you didn't want to check the beach?" his reply seemed fishy to me.

"Ok, ok, I wrote in the log that I checked the beach, but I couldn't once I got there. There was a jumby on the beach. I don't like jumbies." His reply seemed earnest.

I wasn't sure how to respond. If he really believed he saw a ghost on the beach, it would be rude to laugh. Nevertheless, if he really believed that, and he didn't come warn me, what kind of friend was he? This was our security?

"Lamar, aren't you the security guard? Don't you have a gun? Don't you feel the least bit guilty that you didn't try to warn Anna and me?" I decided to take him seriously. Jumby Bay was named for the spirits that were thought to haunt the island.

"I wasn't sure if you knew about jumbies, and I didn't want to scare you. I didn't see you on the beach anyway," he said.

"So, what does a jumby look like, Lamar?" I was genuinely curious about this cultural phenomenon.

"The one I saw tonight was tall and very white. Her dress was flapping in the breeze. She was far away, but I didn't like it. I didn't see you anywhere, so I thought maybe you'd seen it too and left." He didn't seem pleased when I suddenly started giggling. "What's so funny about seeing ghosts?"

"That wasn't a ghost, silly. That was me! I wrapped up in a sheet to keep the bugs from biting me." I had no idea my mosquito defense system would so upset my local friends.

Lamar started chuckling too, and decided to check the beach after all when it was time for my next turtle patrol. He sat with me for the next hour, telling me the legends of Jumby Bay. The island was a sugar plantation until the late 19th century. Rumor has it that the couple that owned the plantation had a troubled marriage. The wife discovered her husband was having an affair with one of the household help. In despair, she hung herself in the Estate House. Her ghost still roams the island, searching for her husband's mistress. I guess Lamar thought I was a vengeful and upset ghost, instead of a turtle girl trying to keep the bugs away.

After a long night without any more jumby sightings, I returned to the house just after sunrise for a short nap. A few minutes later, I heard Lamar's voice calling from the garden, "Hello, the house." When we first arrived, the greeting had seemed so odd, but now we were used to the local regard for privacy. Guests announced their arrival long before walking on the porch to knock on the door.

I walked out to meet Lamar on the porch, knowing he would be uncomfortable entering our house. In his paternal view, he believed two single women should not host a male guest without a chaperone. He had a stack of small cardboard boxes in his hand. "These are for you. Maybe they'll keep the bugs away."

I had to laugh as I looked at his gift – boxes of mosquito coils. Burning them should keep both bugs and jumbies away. "Thanks, Lamar. I hope that means you'll come see us on the beach again too."

****

Two weeks later, it was time for Peach Fuzz to come back to lay another nest. Anna and I packed our bags with snacks, Lamar's mosquito coils, and turtle tags and headed for the beach. As we arrived on the nesting beach, we were surprised to hear "hello" ring out from the top of a tall palm tree.

"Did you hear that?" I asked Anna, not sure if I was imagining things.

"Andy must be around here somewhere." Anna replied, looking about herself warily. Anna was not a fan of strangers on the beach.

Anna and I looked around, trying to find where the voice was coming from. Suddenly, someone pounced down on us from atop a nearby palm tree. Anna screamed, I fell over backwards in the sand, and Andy chortled with glee. Six-foot tall people were not supposed to materialize out of the clear night sky like that, but Andy liked to be unpredictable.

"Are you trying to give us heart attacks?" Anna shrieked at him. Andy was not at all apologetic as Anna and I picked ourselves up and dusted the sand off from our minor tumble on the beach.

"Just wanted to see my American girlfriends…" Andy said as he joined us for our first turtle patrol of the evening. Andy was a charmer, and a good friend to us both. He was another island guard that enjoyed spending time with us on the beach.

After our first walk on the beach revealed that no turtles had arrived yet, we found a few beach chairs to lounge on while we waited until it was time to check the beach again. The rhythms of Andy's island accent blended with the sound of the waves to soothe our nerves and lull us all into a relaxed chat. Anna had brought her portable radio to entertain us through the long night. We listened to the news for a few minutes, catching up on events back home and teaching Andy a bit about life in the US. Since Anna still had her long hair, Andy languidly untangled and braided her windblown locks in tropical island fashion. It seemed like a silent apology for his earlier greeting from the palm tree. As we chatted away, Anna saw another figure walking down the beach. This didn't happen often as most of the guests were at dinner or back in their rooms at this hour.

A voice with a distinct Welsh accent greeted us from a distance, "Are you the infamous turtle girls?"

As the tall, pale woman approached, Anna and I pled guilty to the charge. "Yes, we're the turtle girls. Is there something we can do to help you?" Though we had only been here about six weeks, it was unusual for us to run into someone on the island that we didn't know.

"I'm Nicola – I work for the Franklin's. They thought you might like a snack," she replied as she reached into the small bag she carried with her. "I made too much short bread and mango ice tonight. Would you like to try some?"

"Absolutely," I said as Anna, Andy and I all welcomed our newest friend. We greedily devoured the cookies and sorbet. There were rarely icy desserts of any kind on the island as frozen food melted between the grocery store and the boat ride back to Jumby Bay. This was a rare treat! As we ate, Nicola settled in and told us about how she decided to come to Antigua. She was taking a working holiday as a personal chef away from her home life in Wales. She was hoping the experience would expand her culinary horizons in addition to giving her a much-needed sunny vacation.

With Nicola's Welsh lilt and Andy's island cadence, Anna and I felt very provincial. Our flat Mid-Atlantic accents were dull in comparison. English has so many musical variations, and ours just seemed lacking. Regardless, we were happy to have a new friend join our small group. Not many people stayed on the island for more than six weeks, so having friends who would be here for months was a wonderful gift. We quickly made plans to meet with Nicola the following afternoon to explore the island and our fast friendship.

Soon, it was time to check the beach again.

As we got ready to go, we noticed a crawl on the sand right beside us. There was a turtle somewhere -- maybe it was Peach Fuzz! As Anna and I slowly rose from our chairs, we searched around ourselves for the newly arrived turtle.

"How did that sneaky turtle get by without us noticing?" Anna asked as she looked at the crawl alongside her.

"We were probably too busy talking to notice," Nicola offered.

"No, no, no, you girls were too busy talking. Blah blah blah blah blah… I saw her, I just didn't tell you about the turtle, that's your job," Andy protested, still trying to protect his image as our personal night watchman after scaring us earlier that evening.

"Do you remember hearing about the turtle nesting right under one of these chairs a few years ago? Wouldn't it be funny if that happened tonight?" I replied.

We didn't find her that easily though – this sea turtle had inched right by our chairs without us even seeing her. We decided to check the rest of the beach for other turtle tracks before returning to look more closely for the turtle we had missed. We would be able us to focus completely on finding the quiet turtle that had slipped past us once we knew there were no other turtles on the beach.

Anna, Nicola, Andy and I were determined to find the missing sea turtle. We searched along the sand dunes behind the beach, but we couldn't see her. We crashed through the bushes and mangrove trees. We even tried to find her on the open beach, but we didn't see a turtle anywhere.

"Hey, Andy," I said, "I thought you were the night watchman who sees everything. So where's our turtle?"

Andy shrugged his shoulders. Clearly, this was not his best night.

"How can we lose an animal that's over three feet long?" Anna asked as we continued to search without results. "Kirsten, did you see another crawl heading back to the sea? Maybe she couldn't find a good place to nest and already left."

"I didn't notice anything, but I'll go check again. You would think all the noise we're making would scare her away too." I replied

Sea turtles are often hard to find once they stop moving. They may be hidden among mangrove roots, under leaves or in a pile of seaweed. Sometimes, they accidentally cover themselves with sand as they are digging their nests, so they blend in with the beach. On rare occasions, they crawl to places few sea turtles have ever been before.

It was a very windy night. The shadows of the palm trees danced in the moonlight and the sound of waves and the wind in the trees distracted us. Blowing sand stung our legs as the wind whipped along the beachfront. We searched for another hour and were ready to admit defeat. By now, she should have finished nesting and returned to the sea, but there was no crawl back to the sea anywhere. I didn't know if I was more scared that we had lost her on the beach, or worried that we had missed a nesting event. We had a commitment to every biologist that had ever worked this beach to find every turtle, every time she nested on this beach. Failure was not an option.

Sometimes it helps to have extra eyes searching through the night in the woods, dunes and gardens that edge the beach. It was important not to lose an animal. If this sea turtle was disoriented and stayed on the island after the sun rose, she could get too hot and get sick or even die. We couldn't allow that to happen.

"I just can't find that turtle anywhere, and she doesn't seem to have left the beach," I said as I walked by Anna and Nicola on the beach. "Have you had any luck yet?"

"I can't find her either. We've been outwitted by a sea turtle with a brain the size of a grape," Anna replied. "I think it's time to ask for help."

"You're right. Let's go," I said. Andy silently nodded his head in agreement.

On our way to gather some friends willing to help us find the lost turtle, we walked by a swimming pool that was right next to the sea. It was an unusual pool because it was filled with salt water. The pool surface rippled with tiny waves that we thought were from the trade winds that were blowing strongly that night. We stopped to look anyway, just to enjoy the night and to think of other places where the sea turtle could have wandered.

"Hey you guys, do you see what I see swimming in the pool?" Peach Fuzz was swimming in small circles around the edges.

"That silly turtle! She must have confused the pool with the ocean. It's a pretty small ocean!" Andy said.

Now we had a new problem and we still needed help. How were Anna, Andy, Nicola and I going to get a 140-pound turtle out of the swimming pool without hurting her, or us? She was too heavy to pick up, too fast to catch and she was unable to crawl out on her own. She was born to swim, and she was swimming fast laps around the pool, seeming to search for a way out of the small 'ocean' she was trapped in, but this ocean had no gentle, sloping beach, and four sheer concrete walls. Her powerful flippers were very well adapted for moving quickly through the water, but she couldn't use them to climb the stairs and get back to the beach. For her, there seemed to be no way out.

Trying to catch her might scare her and make her swim even faster as she tried to escape us. She could injure herself hitting or swimming into the walls, handrails and ladders around the pool perimeter. As we stared at her discussing our options, we must have looked like very strange animals to our confused and lost turtle! We quickly attracted the attention of our island neighbors who wondered why we were suddenly fascinated by a swimming pool. A small crowd gathered as more people arrived on the beach to enjoy their evening walks, stopping instead to watch Peach Fuzz. Few people have had the chance to watch a healthy, wild sea turtle so closely.

We had to get Peach Fuzz out of the pool and back in her natural habitat, but we didn't know how. We didn't have any equipment for catching a sea turtle – we were just walking the beach looking for nests. Fishing for sea turtles had been illegal in the country for years, so no one else had any recent professional experience either. We needed a plan. Everyone was eager to help, and offered lots of advice.

Andy asked us, "Why don't you make a sign and show her where the stairs are? Then she can climb out on her own."

"Well," Anna said, trying to hide her smile, "sea turtles can't read."

Nicola called out, "You could try hand signals like a dolphin trainer."

"That might work with some trained animals, but this is a wild sea turtle," I replied. "She probably wouldn't be able to see those signals anyway since she's underwater and we're not. It's also too dark to see well."

"Why don't you just talk to her and tell her how to leave the pool?" someone else suggested.

"We do talk to turtles a lot, but we don't think they understand us," Anna said.

Andy chimed in again, "Why do you have to get her out? Can't she just stay in the pool?"

I said, "It won't hurt her since it's a salt water pool, but it's too small for her to stay in and there's no food for her there."

Finally, Andy came up with a terrific idea. "I have a plan. I'll be back in a minute…" With that, he disappeared, returning a few minutes later with a large white bed sheet. What did Andy have in mind now?

Waving the sheet around him like a matador flagging a bull, Andy said, "If we all work together, we can drag this through the pool like a fishing net. Then, we can pick her up out of the pool."

"That's a great idea. Who wants to help?" Anna asked the crowd. We soon had more help than we knew what to do with.

Six of us worked together to drag the sheet through the water, coaxing the wayward turtle into a corner of the swimming pool. As we came close to catching her, Peach Fuzz dodged our makeshift net and darted to the other end of the pool. We regrouped and tried again, shooing her into another corner. She swam along obediently, then gracefully avoided the net with some impressive underwater gymnastics. She seemed to think the sheet was some sort of predator hunting her.

Peach Fuzz kept swimming away from us for over an hour. It was beginning to feel like an aerobic workout as we continued to chase the turtle with our bed sheet stretched tightly across the width of the pool. Several people stood by the sides of the pool, trying to coach Peach Fuzz and explain to her what was happening. All of our activity woke the mourning doves and bananaquits sleeping in the trees; their startled late-night songs seemed to join the crowd in encouraging Peach Fuzz.

The sheet grew heavy as we continued to drag it against the weight of the water. The muggy night air was stifling and the chase no longer seemed like much fun. Mosquitoes buzzed around our faces and the sheet cut into our hands. We were ready to jump into the pool ourselves, just to cool off a bit, and to get away from the biting insects.

With one final desperate effort, we clumsily drove Peach Fuzz into a corner, trapping her inside the makeshift net. We struggled to heave the cumbersome, frightened and restless turtle out of the water. With her rear flippers hanging out of the net, Peach Fuzz paddled the air furiously, trying to swim through the air as she fought to free herself from the tangled sheet. We worried that we might drop her on the concrete deck, so we huddled closer together to keep her in the fabric while gently setting her on the ground. A cheer erupted from the crowd. I don't think any of us were prepared to wrestle with a sea turtle again anytime soon!

Peach Fuzz had been trapped in there for hours, but she seemed unharmed. We all escorted her back to the beach and let her crawl to the real ocean. Peach Fuzz seemed very agitated after her swim. She left the beach without laying her eggs. We hoped we would see her again later that evening or the next night to attempt to nest again. For now, we were content to know she was safe.

Anna called out, "That was a great idea, Andy! Thanks to all of you for your help!" Andy gathered up his sheet and joined the crowd watching over the very confused Peach Fuzz.

As she was returning to the sea, we tried to explain to Peach Fuzz what had happened, though we knew she couldn't understand us. "You went the wrong way, Peach Fuzz. The beach you want is over there…."

She paid no attention to us at all as she moved back to the ocean as quickly as she could, but her new name stuck. She was Wrong Way Peach Fuzz.

Turtle or Bulldozer?

While Wrong Way Peach Fuzz was busy swimming in the Caribbean, our neighbors decided to build a "turtle fence" behind the first set of dunes. After her unplanned swim, the islanders were worried that turtles might get lost on the island and not find their way back to sea. The fence was meant to prevent sea turtles from crawling through the woods and into the rest of the island. It took a lot of hard work during the heat of the Caribbean summer but no one complained. We didn't want to see one of the turtles get lost again.

Wrong Way Peach Fuzz arrived on the beach later that night and crawled straight towards the spot where she had laid her first nest two weeks earlier. She had not returned to the beach after her adventure the night before, so she still had a full clutch to lay.

Unfortunately, the nesting site she chose was on the other side of the new turtle fence. It was a formidable wooden staked fence, three feet high, tightly woven with vines, and buried deep within the sand dune. It seemed impossible for a turtle to get over, under or through the new barrier. A determined turtle would have to crawl twenty yards down the beach to the end of the fence, and then crawl back up the beach to her chosen spot if she wanted to nest on the other side of the new barrier. Or so we believed.

The fence was a great idea, but it was no match for our new mama turtle. Wrong Way Peach Fuzz was determined to overcome any obstacle placed in her path. We found her new crawl near the base of the sand dune and started to look for the turtle who had created the trail. We quickly found Peach Fuzz on top of the dune. She was doggedly bashing her head against the new fence, tearing it apart, bit-by-bit, with her fore-flippers, forcing her way to her nesting site. We didn't have the heart to stop her. Anna and I were a little afraid that she would attempt to crawl right through us if we tried to move her, so we just sat and watched as she stubbornly continued to break down the barrier that kept her from her chosen spot. After about an hour, she managed to rip a hole in the fence big enough to crawl through. The determined turtle reached her goal, and promptly dug a new nest, right inside her old one.

****

Sea turtles are known for their amazing homing abilities. Scientists believe sea turtles return to the same beach from which they hatched when it is time for them to lay their own eggs. We don't understand exactly how they find this one beach out of the thousands that exist, but they do. In fact, Peach Fuzz was so good at finding her way that she returned to precisely the same spot she had nested in just two weeks earlier. As she was digging, she began uncovering her own developing eggs.

Peach Fuzz had no way of knowing that she had dug up another nest. When sea turtles dig their egg chamber, they use their rear flippers, so they can't see what they're doing. It's unlikely that they would deliberately dig up another nest, but it does happen. On nesting beaches in some parts of Central America, Mexico and India, a more abundant species of sea turtle, the olive ridley, nests in large groups called "arribadas". Sea turtles on these crowded beaches often nest so close together -- and in such high numbers -- that they lay their eggs inside or on top of older nests. Usually, these nests do not survive long enough to hatch. While these particular nests may not have a good chance of survival, the turtles lay so many nests that this is not a significant problem.

The extremely rare Kemp's Ridley sea turtle also nests in arribadas on a remote beach in Rancho Nuevo Mexico, and to a lesser extent, on Padre Island, Texas. Historically, up to 40,000 turtles had been filmed nesting at the same time on these Gulf of Mexico beaches. Hunting pressures, egg poaching and other factors have severely reduced the population of the Kemp's ridley sea turtle and these events are now drastically reduced. As with hawksbill sea turtles like Peach Fuzz, each of these Kemp's ridley nests is now critical to the recovery and survival of this sea turtle species.

Jumby Bay wasn't crowded with turtles, so digging up old nests shouldn't be a problem here. There were over four hundred yards of beachfront for our forty turtles to use as nesting grounds. Sometimes, strange things happened, and we adapted to protect as many nests as possible. We wanted to do our best to promote the survival of hawksbills as a species. Anna and I knew the best thing to do was to create a new nest for the eggs Peach Fuzz was just beginning to lay. We stepped in to catch her new eggs, gently setting them aside in a cooler lined with sand. We would place the eggs in a nest we built nearby. Otherwise, it was unlikely that either nest would hatch.

****

Anna and I took turns using our hands to dig in the sand, attempting to make a new nursery for the precious sea turtle eggs. At first, we dug in sand that was too dry. The sides of the nest caved in before it was deep enough for the turtle eggs, so we had to start over again. The second nest we dug was too close to the water and the sand near the bottom was very wet – too wet to protect the sea turtle eggs for the two months required for their hatching. Mold and mildew can grow in a damp nest, which can cause the eggs to rot before they develop. On our third attempt, we finally got it right.

Scientists believe that sea turtles may use the soft skin on the underside of their necks to help determine if sand has the right amount of moisture for a nest. Anna and I didn't know how to do this, so we were learning to use our own best judgment as we worked. We needed a nest that wouldn't cave in before we placed the eggs inside, as well as one that wouldn't flood during high tides or storms. As humans, we were not very skilled at finding a suitable site.

Anna and I also struggled to dig a deep enough egg chamber with our bare hands. It's hard work digging a sea turtle nest! As we didn't have the two-inch long claws and leathery skin that Peach Fuzz has to help her cut through the roots of beach vegetation, we had to improvise. We used our hands as shovels and picked up seashells to help us cut through plant roots buried deep in the ground. We cut ourselves frequently on the rough sand and rocky bits of coral that were scattered within the beach. We learned to respect Peach Fuzz's efforts even more after we shared in the experience of digging a safe nest for her developing hatchlings.

We were happy to return home after the sun rose that morning. Anna and I put a lot of effort into our artificial nest, and we had sand in places that we never imagined possible. I had sand in my ears, my bellybutton, my teeth, under my fingernails, and in my flashlight. When we had finally shaken it all out of our clothes, we had enough to build a small hill on the kitchen floor. Since we were accumulating so much sand in our island home, Anna and I decided to save the sand and take it back to the beach later that night.

As I stepped into the shower to try to clean the rest of beach off me, Anna yelled that she was headed to the office for a planned chat with her boyfriend. He was working in the Peace Corps in Africa and could only get to a phone once a month. Despite the lack of sleep and the coating of fine sand sticking to her face and legs, she seemed happy as she skipped out the door.

When Anna returned an hour later, her tear-streaked face spoke volumes. I didn't know what to do – should I ask her what happened, or let her have some space to deal with her emotions? I decided to talk to her before we both headed to bed.

"What's wrong, Anna? Did you hurt yourself?" I asked, hoping that was the case, but knowing already that this was something more.

"No, I just had a fight with Sam, and I can't do anything about it. All I can do is write a letter or wait another month for a phone call. I hate this." Anna vented her frustration.

I couldn't imagine how hard it was to have a conflict and not be able to resolve it – I know it would consume me if I were in her shoes. I had no idea how to help her. So, that's what I said. "I'm not very good with these things, so I have no idea what to tell you Anna, other than to say I'm here if you want to talk."

"Thanks, but I think I just need a little space." Anna looked heart-broken and very tired.

"For what it's worth, I'm sure it will work out. He really loves you." I tried to be reassuring, but knew there was little I could do to help. Sometimes, time is the best solution. I hugged Anna and headed to bed, leaving her to sit and write in her journal as Rusted Root played in the background.

When I woke that afternoon, Anna seemed to have bounced back. I wasn't sure if she really had, but I didn't want to upset her by asking. She knew I was there for her, and we had work to do. The beach and the turtles were always waiting for us.

We headed to the beach as usual just before sundown. Anna was subdued, and I made an effort to let her have more space than usual. I knew she was struggling.

When we reached the beach, Anna and I were surprised to see that there were many people tracks on the beach that we didn't recognize. We were so familiar with everyone on the island that used this beach that we were troubled by the numerous footprints. The mystery might be just the thing to pull Anna out of her unhappy thoughts.

"What do you think about that, Anna?" I asked as we walked farther along the beach, following the footprints. "We don't usually see such heavy traffic on this beach, maybe over by the dock or the Estate House, but that's pretty far away."

"Maybe someone had a party or a wedding on the beach today," Anna suggested.

"I guess that's possible – it is a resort in paradise. Do you think we should check with Lamar and Andy anyway? They might be able to tell us what's up, and I'd hate to startle any guests on the beach, or have them scare a nesting turtle."

"That's probably a good idea. Let's head to the guard shack after we check the beach," Anna seemed relieved to have something else to talk about with me.

Once we knew there were no turtles on the beach, Anna and I hopped back on our bikes to go find Lamar or Andy. Both of them were hanging out by the dock, enjoying the cool evening air.

"Hey Lamar, Andy… were there lots of new guests on the boat today?" I shouted as I dropped my bike on the Estate House lawn.

"No, there were only three guests leaving today, no new guests arrived," Andy replied.

"Hmm. That's odd," I said, "There are tons of tracks all over Pasture Bay Beach."

"Really? Are you sure they're not yours?" Lamar asked.

"Come on, Lamar. How long have we been here? Don't you think we recognize our own footprints, and yours and Andy's and Nicola's?" Anna asked incredulously. "There was a big enough group out there that we thought there might have been a party or a wedding."

"That doesn't sound right. You girls stay here, Andy and I are going to check the beach," Lamar said.

While Lamar and Andy patrolled the beach, Anna and I listened to the radio in the guard shack. We both cracked up as "Born in Wadadli," a Calypso version of "Born in the USA," played on the local station. Springsteen would be proud.

Lamar and Andy returned about twenty minutes later, looking very stern. "You girls will have to leave now – go back home. Do not go back to the beach until we come get you. Those tracks could be from turtle hunters, conch fishermen or thieves that are looking for empty houses. Whoever they are, they're up to no good. We're calling the Army."

Only on Jumby Bay would they call the Antiguan Army for footprints that people didn't recognize. Anna and I welcomed the chance for a nap after sundown. Lamar and Andy promised someone would come for us if the Army said it was ok. As soon as we reached the house, I slipped between my sheets, grateful for the unexpected rest, though I worried about missing a turtle. Those worries faded into the distance as sleep arrived, gift-wrapped in the darkness of early evening.

Around midnight, a voice called out from the garden "Hello the house..." the typical island greeting. I rose, startled from my unaccustomed rest, and ran to the door. I was happy I was still in my turtle patrol clothes when I reached the porch and stood face to face with an armed Antiguan military officer.

"Yes, sir, how can I help you?" I stammered, alarmed, as he stood there with a gun slung casually over his shoulder. I have no experience with guns, or police, so I have no idea what kind of firearm he carried so nonchalantly.

"We just wanted to give you the all clear. We've searched the island and can't find anyone here who doesn't belong – whoever was on the beach must have left. You can go look for your turtles now," the officer explained.

Anna had joined us on the porch by then. The skeptical look in her eyes said it all. "You think we're going back on the beach? Would you go back out there tonight without a gun?"

The officer looked at us with a wry smile, "I guess not. If I didn't have a gun and thought there were people out there, I think I'd stay at home. It's up to you though. We didn't see anyone."

"Thanks for letting us know," Anna replied as we bid the officer goodbye. Neither of us could believe the Army had actually gotten on a boat, motored the three miles to Jumby Bay and searched the island just because we saw footprints we didn't recognize. Sure, there were a lot of them, but the response seemed a little extreme.

After talking it over for a few more minutes, Anna and I agreed it might be a good idea to come up with a compromise. While Antigua was very safe, other turtle biologists had encountered problems with aggressive turtle poachers that we hoped to avoid. The

Army likely scared any poachers away, but we didn't want to take any chances. We'd walk the beach one more time together, and then call it an early night.

We went to the beach at first light the next morning and were happy to see there were no turtle tracks from the previous night. We hadn't missed any animals and Anna and I both got the good night's rest we needed after several months of twelve-hour workdays. We hadn't realized just how exhausted we were.

Tree Climbing for Turtles

Anna and I loved Antigua, but working so far from home was hard for the two of us. Anna was still struggling with her long distance relationship with her boyfriend and I longed for my friends and family back home. We always looked forward to news or visitors from the US. We were delighted when Anna's parents decided to visit us and meet the turtle they had heard so much about.

Anna's parents flew down from Pennsylvania to learn about the hawksbills, help us on the beach, and enjoy our island paradise. We were especially happy that Tim and Rebecca were cooking for us. They brought lots of goodies from the United States that we couldn't buy in Antigua. I had been craving graham crackers for weeks, and Anna was happy to have a new supply of M and Ms. It's amazing how such small things could make us feel better when we were missing home. We had found many new favorite foods in the islands too, but nothing beat a snack from childhood. I'd have to worry about finding a supply of Hob Nobs and curry rotis once we went back to the US.

On the night Peach Fuzz was due for her next nest, Tim, Rebecca, Anna and I headed to the beach to look for turtles. Since Peach Fuzz had given us the slip a few times already, we were very thorough in our searches.

Late that evening, I found an in-crawl on the beach, close to the pool Peach Fuzz had taken a swim in just a few weeks before. I spent an hour looking, but I couldn't find a turtle. She wasn't in the bushes, she wasn't under the hammock, and she wasn't lost in the garden. I walked through the cushy beach grass. She wasn't there either. Where had that turtle gone this time? I was getting an uncomfortable sense of déjà vu. I needed help.

I found Anna and her parents farther down the beach, "There's a turtle crawl by the swimming pool, but I can't find a turtle anywhere. It must be Peach Fuzz playing hide-and-seek again."

Anna said, "That silly turtle could be anywhere! Let's split the beach in half – Mom and I will go towards the point. You and my Dad can go look around the pool end of the beach. Maybe she crawled behind the turtle fence in the dunes and got stuck somewhere."

"Sounds like a plan. Let's meet back here in thirty minutes," I said as Anna's father and I left to search our half of the beach.

Tim and Rebecca were excited to be on the beach. They had visited us once in Georgia too, but this was a new experience, traveling to a tropical island to look for our wandering sea turtle. As they already had some sea turtle experience, Tim and Rebecca were very well prepared. They were outfitted like seasoned biologists, with headlamps, mosquito nets, Swiss Army knives, Tevas and bandannas. It was funny to see my friends parents play dress up, but they were well armed against the swarms of mosquitoes that sometimes hunted us on the beach. There was no doubt in my mind that the four of us would find our lost turtle.

As we wandered around the pool, we looked carefully for any signs of a turtle. Tim and I found little bits of turtle tracks in all sorts of different places – in the dirt, on the beach, and in the garden, but we didn't find Peach Fuzz. By now, we knew it had to be her!

After a thorough search of the pool and garden area, Tim and I had to go back to meet Anna and her mother and check the beach again for other turtles; we couldn't let another turtle slip by while we were searching for the missing one. Our nesting beach was an index beach with a saturation-tagging project. That meant it was our responsibility to find and identify every turtle that crawled up and laid a nest on Pasture Bay Beach.

****

Scientists worry that we may have some effect on the turtles we study, so there are usually only a few 'index beaches' in an area. These are the beaches where we make extraordinary efforts to find every single turtle that crawls out of the sea. We never take a night off, call in sick, or leave early, unless there are extreme circumstances. It takes a lot of determination and dedication, and a great love of sea turtles. We leave other beaches without any biologists working through the night, so the turtles are completely undisturbed. Sometimes, scientists walk these beaches after sunrise to count the number of crawls in the sand. This count gives them a good idea of how many turtles visited the beach during the night. The comparison can help us see if we might be bothering the turtles so much that the turtles change their nesting beach.

About two dozen sea turtle biologists had worked on this project at Pasture Bay Beach for over 15 years. It is the longest running, and most comprehensive, study of nesting hawksbills in the world. The information gathered from this beach helps international scientists understand more about how long sea turtles live, how many nests they can lay, and how changes in the beach itself can affect the success of sea turtle nesting. We had a duty to all of these scientists to maintain the high standards of this study as we worked to better understand these ancient and amazing animals.

****

After checking the beach, the four of us walked back through the gardens and grass where I first saw Peach Fuzz' trail. As we neared the golf cart track that rings the island, we noticed leaves on the path. The gardeners sweep it every day, so usually, it's impeccably clean. Maybe this was a clue!

"Peach Fuzz must have been here – look at all the leaves scattered on the path. There aren't any anywhere else on the road," I said, as I scanned the brick sidewalk. We were starting to feel like detectives as we searched for any signs of a sea turtle.

"Let's stop here for a minute and look more closely – maybe she's still near," Anna agreed as we all stopped walking.

Standing silently in the silvery moonlight, we listened to the night for a minute or two. We could hear the wind rattling the palm fronds behind us, the distant hum of a boat engine, and the rhythmic lull of waves gently washing the sandy beach. The scent of frangipani flowers floated on the air from a tree that was in full bloom. Soon, we heard a scratching sound from the other side of the path that didn't fit with the regular pattern of sound. Maybe that was our turtle...

"Did you hear that?" Anna's Mom asked us all. "There it is again. There's some kind of animal nearby." Rebecca had many pets at home and was well attuned to the signs of animals.

"There aren't many animals out at this time of night, though there are a few stray cats on the island. Maybe it's the missing turtle," I said as we all tried to determine where the sound was coming from.

Anna turned on her flashlight and peered along the edges of the path "See that? The cactus is crushed as if someone walked through it. Do you think a sea turtle could do that?"

"With that turtle, I think anything is possible," Anna's father, Tim, replied.

Using all of our flashlights to scrutinize the edge of the woods, we found Peach Fuzz. She had crawled through the cactus and was starting to make her way over a small bush where she seemed to be stuck. One flipper was caught on a low-lying branch and the other was waving in the air, as if she were trying to say hello to a friend, or maybe get our attention.

"Well that's a first. I've never seen a sea turtle try to climb a tree before!" I said as we all chuckled over Peach Fuzz's unusual predicament.

"Well, let's go get her! Watch out for cactus spines..." Anna warned as we all began to walk into the woods to retrieve the adventurous sea turtle.

It would take all four of us – Anna, her parents and I – to pick up the 140-pound turtle and bring her back to the path. Peach Fuzz was tangled in the small sea grape she had started to climb, so we had to cut her out of the tree carefully to avoid harming her. Tim was skillful with his Swiss Army Knife, and set to work trimming the small tree to free our turtle. Anna, Rebecca and I held Peach Fuzz still so Tim could get to work without being hit in the face with a rogue sea turtle flipper. I think Peach Fuzz was mad enough to smack him, even if it would have been an accident.

Once she was free, we still had to find a way to walk through the cactus patch, in sandals, carrying an angry, thrashing sea turtle that was determined to get away from us. We used all our muscle to keep the turtle still, but she continued to squirm in our arms. We worried she might wriggle out of our grasp and drop on the cactus.

There was no time for a plan – we simply had to get through the cactus and examine Peach Fuzz for injuries. So, four tired, clumsy adults tiptoed quickly through the cactus with an agitated sea turtle. It must have been a very strange sight. Once we reached the path, we carefully turned her on her back to check for cactus spines before taking the cactus spines out of our own feet. We didn't want to send her back to the sea with splinters in her skin. Peach Fuzz had not laid her eggs yet, but we doubted she would lay them after being so disoriented. We decided to take her back to the beach and let her return to the safety of the sea. She had had quite a night!

The next night, we were certain Peach Fuzz would return. Since there were four of us while Anna's parents were in the country, we decided to spread ourselves along the beach so we could see Peach Fuzz as she emerged from the sea. Under the light of the full moon that night, we could even see turtles swimming along the limestone fore-reef, searching for a way to get to the beach.

Anna sat in front of Banaquit, the house with the pool where Peach Fuzz had been trapped a few weeks before. Around ten o'clock, Anna let out a loud screech, getting everyone's attention. Thinking the wily sea turtle had arrived and was in trouble again, Rebecca, Tim and I all ran across the sand to find Anna flailing her arms and cursing mildly under her breath. "Those fire ants are everywhere!"

"Fire ants?" I asked, "Where did they come from? Are you on an ant nest?"

"I was hungry, so I thought I'd have a snack. When I reached into my backpack to get my bagel, there were ants everywhere. This island is overrun with ants..."

Anna and I were plagued with sugar ants back at the house. Their constant presence while they searched for food in the kitchen had aggravated us to no end. Now, we stored the sugar and cereal in the freezer and adopted Dave Matthews "Ants Marching" as our theme song. A sense of humor goes a long way when you're working in a new environment.

Sugar ants didn't bite though. Fire ants bit until your skin blistered and burned. Their bites could be itchy, red welts in minutes. I felt bad for Anna as she ran to the sea to drown the ants that were crawling all over her arms. I laughed as she walked back to us, soaked to the skin but free of ants.

"So, are you still hungry?" I had to ask. Anna glared at me and asked her parents if they wanted to stop at the house for a critter-free snack after we checked the beach. We all thought that was a good idea.

Peach Fuzz didn't show up until after midnight. With four of us to shepherd her on the beach, she managed to lay her eggs and return to the sea without incident. If only was had so much help every time she came to shore!

An Uninvited Guest

Hurricanes are a common occurrence in the Caribbean Sea in the summer, though it was one experience that Anna and I hoped we would miss. In mid-September, we learned we would not be so lucky. There was a hurricane spinning across the Atlantic Ocean.

John, our lawyer and island father, made a rare call to the island four days before the hurricane was forecast to pass by Antigua. "Hi girls. How are you enjoying your Caribbean year? Sarah and I haven't seen you at the house lately – you know you're always welcome." John sounded tinny and far away through the speakerphone.

"Thanks John," Anna replied. "We've just been so busy with the turtles and teaching that we haven't had time to visit, though I really enjoyed my time there when my parents were visiting."

"We were happy to have you! Sarah loves having guests to feed." John paused, as if preparing himself for a more meaningful message. "I'm sure you and Kirsten have heard about the tropical weather forecast. Hurricane Georges will be passing by the area soon."

"Yeah, we've been keeping an eye on every hurricane this year. I can't believe how many there are! Doesn't it stress you out to have to deal with them all the time?" Anna replied.

"They really don't hit Antigua all that often – maybe once every ten years. Things can be a mess then, but it's the price you pay for living in paradise...," John paused for a moment. "It looks like Georges won't be much of a threat though – it's forecast to pass north of us as a Cat I or II. Nothing to worry about."

"That may be true in your world, John, but I'm not used to hurricanes passing through the neighborhood," Anna said. "Do you think we need to call Jim and see if he wants us to evacuate to Trinidad or the US?"

"I really don't think it's that much of an issue. You're more than welcome to come spend a few days with Sarah and me if you'd feel more comfortable here."

"Give us a little while to talk about that. It sounds like a great option, but it might be better just to stay here with the turtles if the storm doesn't look that bad. Can we get back to you later this afternoon?" Anna asked for both of us.

Anna and I talked about John's offer and consulted the weather forecast on the internet. All the predicted hurricane tracks went about a hundred miles north of the island, so we felt safe staying on Jumby Bay. As long as the winds, waves and lightning weren't bad, we wouldn't even have to miss the night on the beach. Peach Fuzz was due back for her next nest near the day the storm was expected to hit. We knew we had to keep ourselves safe during the hurricane, but we felt secure in the shelter Jumby Bay provided.

Anna called John back and declined his offer – we were going to ride out the storm on Jumby Bay. We were anxious about our decision, but we believed we made the right choice.

Anna and I followed the weather forecasts obsessively over the next few days. Hurricane Georges stalled east of Antigua, and gathered strength as it churned over the warm sea. Over the next two days, we prepared the island for high winds, torrential rain and crashing waves. We gathered all the beach chairs, umbrellas, rafts, and beach toys and stored them in sturdy buildings on high ground.

Andy and Lamar taught us how to use cement nails and plywood to board up windows. Nicola and the Franklins went home to the UK, leaving their vacation home in the care of their housekeeper. We closed the storm shutters on our small teak and tile house and moved all of our satellite transmitters and computers to the strongest building we could find. We gathered our clothes, music and everything else and stored them in the bathtub under an old mattress.

I was grateful to have so much work to do. I didn't want anyone, especially Anna, to know how scared I was. I felt I'd done the wrong thing by insisting we stay on the island during the storm, and I was ashamed to admit I'd made a mistake. I think Anna was as scared as I was, but we didn't really talk about it – we just poured all of our nervous energy into getting ready for the storm. As we walked the beach later that night, dark beach and crashing waves were a soothing respite for our tired nerves.

****

Neither Anna nor I was sure staying on Jumby Bay was the best choice. Hurricanes are deadly storms – the tidal surges, wind, rain, flying coconuts and other debris destroy property, topple buildings and take lives. As the storm closed in on us, the reality of its terribly violent power sunk in. The morning before the storm was expected, Andy and Lamar prepared to take all of the boats from Jumby Bay over to the main island of Antigua. They would tie them up among the mangrove trees to protect them from the storm surge.

I'd never felt so isolated in my life – our one link to John, the main island and the illusion of safety and home sailed away with

Lamar and Andy. There were now only eleven people on the island. Like it or not, we were stuck there until the sea was calm enough for our small island boats to return.

It was small consolation to know we had everything we would need. Before he left, Andy had worked hard to keep us laughing. He encouraged us to throw a hurricane party to help us bond with the few people remaining on Jumby Bay. We had to eat all the ice cream, desserts and other treats in the resort kitchen since they would all go bad when we lost power during the storm. That was the best part of getting ready for a hurricane.

As the storm strengthened, Hurricane Georges made an unexpected turn, heading directly for Antigua. The situation had changed quickly, and Anna and I grew more fearful. We knew there was no way we could leave our three-hundred acre island – it was our entire world until after the storm passed. Television news cameras had shown us the damage hurricanes were capable of creating. We had no idea what madness the impending storm would bring into our lives. Our other friends on the island were starting to get frightened too, but everyone tried to laugh it off. There was nothing we could do. Anna and I called our parents in the US to let them know that we were in a safe place, and that we may not be able to call for many days. We didn't want them to worry about us and we knew they would be watching the news. I think we were more concerned about our families than we were about ourselves.

****

The next day dawned bright and beautiful with no sign of the storm headed our way, other than unusually rough waves on the beach. In late morning, a traffic jam of grey clouds piled onto the blue horizon; by mid-afternoon, they crowded out the island sun with their towering, blackened height. Rain bands, gusty winds and thunderstorms started to arrive in the late afternoon. The eleven of us on the island decided it was time to barricade ourselves inside our storm shelter.

The safest place to stay during the storm was the 250-year-old Estate House that had been built when the island was a sugar plantation. The building had been renovated since the colonial era, and was still one of the strongest shelters on our small island. Somehow, it had already survived two hundred years of tropical weather in one piece. We each took a few minutes to look around the island before locking ourselves inside. We didn't know what Jumby Bay would look like the next day after Georges had passed.

Just before sealing the doors in our hurricane shelter, we all made one more attempt to connect with friends and family through the internet. We knew it was likely that we would lose power soon, and the short emails soothed our screaming nerves. I checked a local weather bulletin board to see what other Antiguans were saying about Georges. The mixture of indignation, good wishes and island humor was reassuring. I was happy to see messages from so many familiar names – it amazed me that I already had dozens of friends in this small country. Then I read a message that unleashed all of my pent up fear.

"I can't believe we're looking into the face of God so soon after Hurricane Luis." I had never heard John speak in such ominous tones. Now I knew it was okay to be afraid. I hesitated to show the note to Anna, but I knew she had a right to see what John was thinking. We looked at each other, finally allowing our fears to show. Anna and I cried as we hugged each other. We knew we were safe, but the fear of the unknown monster at the door was overwhelming.

The air inside quickly grew still and hot as the storm outside took down power lines and we lost our air conditioning and lights. The windows were all sealed against the wind and driving rain, so there wasn't a breath of air in the coral rock building. It felt as if we were trapped in a small and shrinking drum, with the storm steadily beating at the edges. It was going to be a long night.

We huddled in the darkness, listening to the shrieking winds and the rain pounding on the thick walls surrounding us, grateful to be warm and dry. Anna had brought her portable radio and a stack of batteries so we could listen to books-on-tape as the storm raged outside. It was reassuring to laugh as we listened to the soothing voice of the anonymous reader, telling amusing tales of family and friends. His stories, our bowls of melting ice cream, and the companionship of the others gathered around the radio were the only things that seemed normal that night.

When there was a lull in the storm around midnight, Anna peeked outside our shelter to see what the island looked like. She stood at the one unbolted door and beckoned to me to follow her. It was wonderful to breathe in the cool, rain-soaked air and feel the light breeze on my face, but it was not a good idea to stay outside until we knew the hurricane was over.

After about twenty minutes, the relative stillness was disturbed by the sound of an approaching train. At first, Anna and I were confused – there we no trains at all in Antigua! We soon realized this was the sound of the hurricane re-approaching as the calm of the eye slipped away and the winds started to blow again from the opposite direction. We stepped back inside the safety of our prison-like shelter to wait out the rest of the storm.

The winds were relentless as they tore across the island all through the long night. Some of the plywood boards we had nailed over the windows loosened, and banged a steady rhythm against the thick coral rock walls. Several pieces of the roof tore off and rain was leaking in. Anna and I tried to sleep on high kitchen counters to keep ourselves dry, but it was hard to get any rest on the cold steel counters while we worried about the weather. We worried about our turtles too, but knew they were likely safe in deep offshore waters; they seem to have a built in weather warning system that kept them from nesting during hurricanes. It was a sleepless night for everyone, as we all silently sat with our own fears.

After the storm winds stopped blowing and the sun emerged from behind the clouds the next morning, we left our sealed-off shelter. Though we had been safe during the storm, we felt as drained as if we had battled it through the night. We were relieved to know the worst was over.

We walked outside to see that Hurricane Georges had destroyed much of our beautiful island. The lush tropical gardens were smashed. There was standing water everywhere. Acacia leaves and palm fronds carpeted the soaked lawns. The tennis courts were underwater, and there was a fig tree on the net. The resort flagpole was bowing down, nearly touching the ground.

Anna and I knew we had to check our nesting beach, though we were reluctant to face the damage we imagined we would find.

"Come on, Anna, let's get it over with," I said as I retrieved my bike from the Estate House shelter.

"Ok, but I'm not so sure I'm ready for this," Anna replied.

Our fellow cast-aways tried to keep us from leaving the general area. No one knew what we might find on the short ride to Pasture Bay Beach. There was a real possibility of looters, and further danger from the unknown debris and destruction we would encounter near the shore. We were determined to check our nests, no matter what unknown hurdles may be in our way.

Anna and I carefully wound our way around fallen trees, crumbled walls, scraps of plywood and plastic, tumbled furniture and a wrecked fiberglass boat hull. Debris was strewn across the entire island, making the four-minute ride take over half an hour.

When we arrived at the nesting beach, we knew there was little hope of finding a surviving nest. A wide trench passed through the middle of the beach, with a swift new river draining all the rainwater from the storm. The ocean front forest of sea grapes and mangroves had rolled over, with the trees freed roots reaching to the sky above. Even the beachside pool was filled with sand.

After a quick survey, we were convinced there were no adult turtles trapped in the wreckage, but we saw scattered turtle eggs and hatchlings everywhere. It was too depressing to stay on the beach. We needed to get away from the destruction and check on our home and our friends as well.

We looked in awe at how our newly adopted home had changed overnight. We hardly recognized it! Our favorite flamboyant trees were split right in half. There was corrugated tin wrapped around tree trunks and boats sailing on dry ground. The porch and roof on our home was gone; there were only a few walls leaning at odd angles, with shattered windows, as evidence of our former home. We didn't see or hear any birds singing. It wasn't what we had expected to see. Mother Nature was clearly more powerful than we could understand.

As the seas calmed a little, Andy and Lamar returned to the island with the resort boats and news of the main island. Many of our friends, including Andy, had lost their homes, but everyone we knew was safe. Andy had been in his house when the hurricane straps broke and the modest island home literally rolled down the hill. How terrifying that must have been! An estimated thirty to forty percent of the country was destroyed, with entire towns washed away by the storm surge. Georges was much worse than any of us expected a few days earlier.

Antigua is a very welcoming place, and everyone helped their neighbors in any way they could. Families without homes quickly found shelter, parceling children out among family members. Most of Andy's family had arranged to stay with family and friends in the area. The newly homeless were already banding together, drawing up plans to rebuild the island one home at a time. Andy chose to stay on our small island and help rebuild the gardens and buildings that were damaged here.

We had a lot of work to do before we could head to the beach that night, so we hopped on our bikes, rode around the island and did what we could to help our friends and neighbors clean-up. We spent a long afternoon picking up banana bunches that had fallen from the trees, gathering splintered fiberglass from shattered boats, picking up pieces of furniture and roof tiles, and surveying the damage to our home and the other island buildings. Our biggest problems after the storm were that we had no fresh water, no power and a lot of damage to the buildings. We were all very lucky though; everyone was safe and we could all work together to repair or replace what was broken.

After the sun set at the end of the day, we went to visit Pasture Bay Beach to see if any turtles would crawl out of the sea that night. We weren't sure how the hurricane might have affected them and didn't know what to expect.

Walking the beach was a challenge that night as there was debris from the storm everywhere. Anna and I tripped over boat sails, oars, seat cushions, fishing nets, beach umbrellas, fallen trees and other debris as we walked the first section of the beach. We agreed to go in opposite directions, each covering half of the beach so we could find any nesting or lost sea turtles faster. All of the uprooted trees, wood, tin and other trash on the beach would make it more difficult for the turtles to nest and much easier for them to get lost or trapped in the tangled mess.

It was a heart-breaking night. All of the nests that our turtles had so carefully created over the past four months were gone. The storm had reshaped the beach and destroyed every nest. We found many eggs in the surf, trapped in fallen branches and scattered among the storm debris, but we knew they would never hatch.

It was time for some good news.

While walking near a broken palm tree, my head bent with the sorrow and fatigue of the last few days, I noticed the large number of beautiful shells that had washed up with the storm. I started to collect these, thinking they would make nice souvenirs for my family back in the States. I had never seen such perfect shells, or so many. They seemed to be a gift from the storm tossed sea that had washed away so much of our nesting beach.

I quietly worked my way down the beach, watching for turtles and shells. A smile slowly spread across my face when I noticed a fresh turtle crawl in the sand. Following the trail higher up the beach, I saw a sea turtle starting to lay her eggs, near the sand-filled swimming pool. At first, I could hardly believe my eyes. After checking her flipper tags to be sure, I knew this was Peach Fuzz. I called out to Anna, "You'll never guess who's on the beach!"

"No way! I guess Wrong Way finally found the right way back to the beach," Anna laughed.

We sat beside Peach Fuzz, enjoying the warmth of the late summer evening and talking about all of her escapades that summer. We were happy to be back to relatively normal tasks. Wrong Way Peach Fuzz had kept us on our toes and taught us to expect the unexpected. Hopefully, her next nesting visit would not be quite so exciting.

Tracking Peach Fuzz

Anna and I were anxious for Peach Fuzz to return to the nesting beach. She had already nested several times during the summer and it was possible that she was finished for the year. If she did return for another nest, Anna and I planned to use a new high-tech tag on her.

Our beach had joined a Caribbean wide satellite-tracking project. The National Marine Fisheries Service in the US gave us five transmitters to use on Jumby Bay turtles. This was a great opportunity to see where our turtles went after they finished nesting for the year. We thought Peach Fuzz would be an interesting neophyte turtle to study. We would use the rest of our transmitters on turtles that had been nesting on Jumby Bay for many years. These turtles are called "remigrants". Remigrants represent a stable group of turtles that return to the same nesting beach every two to three years.

****

In recent years, scientists have started to use satellite transmitters to track the movement of sea turtles after they leave their nesting beach or foraging ground. Sea turtles are hard to find in the wide oceans without this modern technology. These small transmitters send a signal to satellites orbiting the earth. The satellites transmit the information back to us with latitude and longitude readings each time the turtle surfaces to breathe. Each of these points is represented by a dot on a chart of the seas. When you connect the dots, you can follow the path the turtle takes and see where the turtle travels. Using this technology, scientists have found that sea turtles can swim very long distances – even across the ocean.

I spent a week with a team of scientists in Barbados learning how to attach these black plastic boxes to a sea turtle carapace. Anna ran the turtle beach alone for the entire week. Though I greatly appreciated her willingness to take over our responsibilities, I still worry that I may have forgotten to say "thank you" to her for her efforts. If I did forget, here's a very belated and much deserved "Thanks, Anna!"

The transmitters that we used in Antigua were relatively small, about the size of a paperback book. The transmitters were a great idea. They allowed us to track turtles without adding a lot of weight or drag on their shells. Attaching them took some time, but it was necessary to ensure they stayed attached for the year or two the turtles would swim in the world oceans before returning to their nesting beaches.

To protect the turtle scutes from the hard plastic transmitter, we first create an elastomer plastic base as a 'cushion' on the turtle's carapace. The transmitter is then firmly attached to the top of the turtle shell with fiberglass strips and a glue-like substance called "resin". These are the same materials used to repair surfboards and boats. The turtle has to remain on the beach for several hours as we complete the tagging process. We release the turtle as soon as the resin on the transmitter is dry.

****

Two weeks after the hurricane, Peach Fuzz arrived back on Pasture Bay Beach in the same spot where she laid her first nest. This time, she didn't have to break through the turtle fence as it was destroyed in the storm. Maybe the fence wasn't such a great idea in the first place. Once Peach Fuzz started to lay her eggs, Anna and I checked her for injuries. We then placed a four-sided wooden box around her. The box was about 4 feet long by 3 feet wide, and made of four boards nailed together, with no bottom and no top. We used the box to keep her still while we attached the satellite transmitter. It's an easy process, but it took a long time.

Shortly after the sun rose, Peach Fuzz was ready. It had taken about five hours to apply the new tag. When we lifted the box to set her free, she raced towards the ocean faster than I had ever seen a sea turtle move. She must have been confused and angry to find herself trapped on the beach for so long!

The next day, Anna and I started to get emails that showed us the 'hits' from Peach Fuzz's new transmitter. These 'hits' are latitude and longitude readings from the satellite that picked up the transmitter signal. Using these readings, Anna and I looked at the map and saw that Peach Fuzz was still very nearby. Not all of the readings were accurate. Sometimes, there was one hit that was far off or that wasn't a strong signal. We didn't use these points because they were not precise enough for our study.

Anna and I were eager to check our email every few days to see where Peach Fuzz had wandered. We didn't think she would be back on our nesting beach this year. We tried to choose turtles for satellite tags that were close to their last nests because the batteries on the transmitters only last about six months. Anna and I wanted to know the turtles were finished nesting and traveling for as many of these months as possible.

After a few weeks, I noticed something strange in Peach Fuzz's readings. "Hey Anna, come look at this. Am I reading this right? Is Peach Fuzz still so close by?"

In our emails, we had tracked four other turtles that had left our nesting beach and traveled to nearby countries, including St Kitts and Nevis and St. Lucia. Peach Fuzz, however, seemed to stay in one place.

"I think you are reading it right. She hasn't been on the beach, has she?" Anna asked.

"I haven't seen her, and I haven't seen any crawls that we missed. I think she really has finished nesting."

"I do too," Anna paused to think, "What do you think this means?"

"It looks like she doesn't want to swim very far away. Maybe we need a more accurate map of the sea. She could be farther away than we think."

All the hits we had for Peach Fuzz showed that she hadn't traveled far at all. In fact, it appeared that she was living on the other side of our island. We hadn't seen her on the nesting beach and there weren't any crawls on the other beaches, so we assumed she was finished nesting. We started to keep our eyes open wide any time we were on the island boat.

One day, Andy was piloting the boat when Anna and I were headed to the main island to go grocery shopping. "Hey, Andy, have you seen any turtles swimming around here?" Anna asked.

"I see turtles all over the place. Keep your eyes on the water!" Andy was still giving us a hard time.

"We're looking for an adult turtle. Did you see the satellite transmitters we were putting on?" I asked.

"You mean those little black boxes? Sure, I watched you put one of them on a few weeks ago." Andy replied.

"We think one of those turtles is swimming around here. Have you seen her?" Anna said.

"Now that you mention it, I have. There's a turtle that hangs out on the reef, just off the boat dock near the Estate House." Andy was happy to have solved our mystery.

I was excited by this news. "Really? Can you let us know if you see her again? We think that's Wrong Way Peach Fuzz."

"Wrong Way? That turtle still doesn't follow the rules!" Andy laughed.

Once again, Peach Fuzz had tricked us. We saw her later that day on our way back to Jumby Bay. She was swimming near the surface, her head just breaking the water as she lifted it to breathe. A foot behind her orangey-brown head, the small black antenna of the satellite transmitter rose above the water. It was fulfilling, in a small way, to see the system functioning in real life. The transmitter sent a signal each time the turtle came up for a breath of air. We would check our email tomorrow to see the position Peach Fuzz's transmitter just relayed to the Argos satellites orbiting the earth.

Though Anna and I walked the beach for several more months, we didn't see Wrong Way Peach Fuzz again. Many island guests reported seeing her on the reef as they snorkeled nearby. Maybe she was so used to attention from people that she wanted to stay near the island for company. She had finished her first nesting season and had succeeded in surprising us at every turn.

Anna and I did look forward to finding her hatchlings. Peach Fuzz's nest by the swimming pool was the first to survive the storm that hit Antigua. It was hard to wait the necessary sixty days for the eggs to develop. On the night that we expected her nest to hatch, we invited Peach Fuzz's friends to come to the nest site to greet her hatchlings. Everyone was eagerly anticipating watching the tiny animals on their hectic dash to the sea.

Under the light of the midnight moon, one hundred golf-ball-sized sea turtle hatchlings boiled from the nest that their mother, Peach Fuzz, had built for them. The hatchlings scattered in all directions, crawling over each other and everything in their paths as they headed to the sea. The crowd laughed as we watched their clumsy race to the water. It was a happy sight!

We didn't know who would be here in twenty or thirty years when these turtles returned to this beach to nest, but we hoped they would be people who would love the turtles, and Antigua, as much as we did.

Glossary

Antigua – a Caribbean nation in the eastern Leeward Islands.

Arribada – a large cohort, usually Kemp's or Olive Ridleys, nesting together on the same beach at the same time.

Carapace – the top shell of a sea turtle.

Clutch – the eggs a sea turtle lays in a nest.

Hawksbill – *Eretmochelys imbricata*; a critically endangered sea turtle species found in tropical oceans worldwide. The hawksbill has a hawk-like beak for feeding on sponges.

Kemp's Ridley – *Lepidochelys kempii*; the smallest sea turtle, found in the Gulf of Mexico and western Atlantic Ocean. Historically nested in arribadas, even during the day, primarily in Rancho Nuevo, Mexico. Currently nests in small numbers in Mexico and other sites, most notably, Padre Island, Texas.

Plastron – the bottom shell of a sea turtle.

Scute – the keratinized scales that form the outer layer of the carapace of most sea turtle species. Leatherbacks are the only extant sea turtles without scutes.

Sea Turtle Information

www.seaturtle.org – a compendium of information, research and updates on sea turtle activity around the world

www.cccturtle.org – general sea turtle information, sea turtle adoption and satellite tracking information, information on classroom projects and educational programs

http://www.turtles.org/ -- general information; highlights information on green sea turtles and fibropapilloma in Hawaii.

http://www.seaturtlehospital.org/ -- the Karen Beasley sea turtle hospital on Topsail Island, NC

http://www.seaturtle.org/mtn/ -- The Marine Turtle Newsletter – the most current information from scientists in the field, available online and in print

http://www.worldwildlife.org/ -- The World Wildlife Fund site – information on sea turtles and other imperiled animals and habitats, and easy ways you can help

Further Reading

The Sea Turtle: So Excellent a Fishe by Archie Carr

The Windward Road by Archie Carr

Time of the Turtle by Jack Rudloe

Sea Turtles: A Complete Guide to Their Biology, Behavior and Conservation by James Spotila

The Biology of Sea Turtles by Peter Lutz, John Musick, and Jeannette Wyneken

Voyage of the Turtle: In Pursuit of the Earth's Last Dinosaur by Carl Safina

Little Turtle and the Song of the Sea by Sheridan Cain and Norma Burgin

Into the Sea by Alix Berenzy

Carolina's Story: Sea Turtles Get Sick Too! By Donna Rathmell and Barbara Bergwerf

Acknowledgements

So many people helped make this book possible. Jim Richardson and his family continue to inspire and educate young biologists through the Jumby Bay Hawksbill Project and the Little Cumberland Island Loggerhead Project. Their dedication and hard work have touched the lives of countless young scientists, nature enthusiasts and inquisitive children of all ages. Rebecca Bell is a driving force behind both projects, and provides much comfort and direction for new turtle people, including a warm welcome at Manana Manor. John and Sarah Fuller and their family give the Antigua turtle teams the guidance, friendship and foundation necessary to succeed in a new country.

My colleague in Antigua, Jordanna Henry, and her parents Tim and Ann, provided me with both family and a steering rudder when I lost direction. Without them and Peach Fuzz, I may never have found my own way home.

Many friends have sustained me with their kindness and patience over the years, most notably: Jorge, Bryn, Londa, Patty, Geary, Rebecca, Kofi, Emmanuel, Sandy, Andrea and Walt. They loved me even when I could not love myself.

As always, I thank my family, especially my younger and wiser sister, Megh, my brothers, Peter and Sean, and my mother, Mary, for their continued support and love throughout both good times and bad. I love you all.

Made in the USA
Middletown, DE
09 August 2015